Masao Furuyama

TADAO ANDO
*1941

The Geometry of Human Space

TASCHEN

Illustration page 2 ► Portrait of Tadao Ando, 2004
Illustration page 4 ► Church of the Light, Ibaraki,
Osaka, Japan, 1987–1989, drawing

© 2006 TASCHEN GmbH
Hohenzollernring 53, D-50672 Köln
www.taschen.com

Editor ► Peter Gössel, Bremen
Design and layout ► Gössel und Partner, Bremen
Project management ► Swantje Schmidt, Eike
Meyer, Bremen
Copy editor ► Christiane Blass, Cologne
Translation from Japanese of the introduction
► Linda Hoaglund, New York
Translation from Japanese of the house
descriptions ► Hiroshi Watanabe, Tokyo

Printed in Germany
ISBN 978-3-8228-4895-1

To stay informed about upcoming TASCHEN
titles, please request our magazine at
www.taschen.com/magazine or write to
TASCHEN America, 6671 Sunset Boulevard,
Suite 1508, USA-Los Angeles, CA 90028,
contact-us@taschen.com, Fax: +1-323-463.4442.
We will be happy to send you a free copy of our
magazine which is filled with information about
all of our books.

Contents

Introduction

Début as a professional boxer, 1958

Long after becoming the world's Ando, Tadao Ando remains even now Osaka's Ando. When he walks down the streets of his native city, people greet him spontaneously. His lectures attract a passionate following. He casually engages students, housewives and taxi drivers in conversation, gladly shaking their hands and signing autographs. Also in Asia, Europe and in America, crowds throng to his lectures and rock with laughter. Yet the secret of Ando's popularity has a great deal to do with his personality. He approaches every project, regardless of its scope, like an animal that has staked its life on capturing its prey. He seems to win life's brutal battles and achieve glory, only to cast it aside and race alone into the distance. This is his singular charm.

Ando ponders his personal experiences, adds intelligent ideas, and then incorporates them into his very essence. He is convinced that experience alone is his only valid weapon. In other words, that it is impossible to move others with mere knowledge, unaided by experience. He is unmoved by architecture that springs entirely from the intellect. He hates the manipulation of knowledge and games with form. For Ando, true architecture is not space expressed through metaphysics or aesthetics, but space that embodies physically absorbed wisdom. In this sense, he seeks neither beautiful nor skillful architecture. He values only intrepid architecture defined by its victory over dilemma, suffering and fear. Because unlike surface beauty, the only expression that invokes sublime emotions in the beholder is that on which a creator stakes his or her life. Behind this lies Ando's belief that life is a constant struggle and that only conflict can incite passion.

A transparent geometry governs Ando's work. It is clear but far from simple. It profoundly reflects the way he has lived his life, his philosophy, and his past experience. It provokes architectural awe.

I believe that Ando's youthful experiences as a professional boxer and childhood experiences at home form the most significant influences on his movement toward architecture.

Ando describes his view of boxing and his own experiences as a 17-year-old boxer in this way: "Boxing is a combat sport in which you rely only on yourself. In the months preceding a bout, you dedicate yourself to training body and mind through practice and fasting. It is a draconian sport on which you gamble your life, embracing both solitude and glory. My experiences as a boxer, the intensity of leaping into the ring, the loneliness of having to fight utterly by oneself, relying on no one, became my creative touchstone."

After choosing architecture, Ando traveled the world in order to research and experience various buildings and spaces, but perhaps no structures influenced him more than the row houses of Osaka's Asahi Ward, where he grew up. Ando has written of his experiences there: "After World War II, I lived in a narrow, oblong, wooden two-story row house with my grandmother, who ran a small shop from her home. Winters were so cold you could practically see the wind race through, and summers were stiflingly hot, admitting no breeze. That home was infuriating in summer and winter

Left page:
The atelier in Oyodo, 1989
Like a deep well between concrete wall and book wall. Ando's seat is at the bottom.

alike. But living there, I grew enraged at society and felt inspired to improve living conditions. I feel that my experiences in that house provide crucial fuel for my creative energy." The architecture of Ando's personality is the very space he inhabited as a child.

Ando's debut project, Row House, Sumiyoshi, perfectly embodies the twin experiences of the architect's youthful boxing career and a childhood in one of Osaka's less-than-affluent *shitamachi* row houses.

Yet the question remains, do architectural works resemble their creators? In other words, is architecture an allegory of its maker? Generally, when discussing architecture, it is taboo to base criticism on personal impressions. However, Ando himself asserts, "Architecture resembles the architect," and architecture inevitably betrays something of its creator's character. A Japanese adage holds, "The style is the man," so, too, "Architecture is the man." Does the Sumiyoshi Row House, then, actually reflect Tadao Ando?

Ando named his dog Corbusier and he and his wife adored the pet. Now deceased, he went by the nickname "Corbu." Ando is hopelessly vulnerable to wounded creatures. He loved dogs as a child, so much so that he used to take his own pet to elementary school. Ando is both a tough architect with a cool critical eye and a deeply humane person who is gentle towards people and loving towards animals. Raymond Chandler once put the following words into Philip Marlowe's mouth: "If I wasn't hard, I wouldn't be alive. If I couldn't ever be gentle, I wouldn't deserve to be alive." The key to Ando's style of "hard-boiled" lies in his cool ability to differentiate between being tough and being loving.

Let us return to impressions of the Sumiyoshi Row House. The first impression is of mystery. Its façade reveals no familiar architectural elements such as windows, roof, or eaves, creating the sense of a non-residential structure, despite the fact that it is a dwelling. The building's indeterminate structure provokes curiosity and discomfort.

Further, the narrowly confined entryway suggests a cantankerous spirit that may angrily deny access. Reminiscent of the low entrance of a traditional teahouse, the

The house where Tadao Ando grew up with his grandmother
The most influential building for young Ando

doorway forces contact with the surrounding concrete, stimulating the sense of touch. But the surface beauty of the concrete is striking and contact with it reveals the depth of its underlying craft. It evokes the simultaneous experience of delicate touch and the centripetal sensation of entering a cave. These dualities of delicacy and strength, kindness and rejection epitomize Ando himself: his hard-boiled aesthetics, his toughness and his love.

Tadao Ando was born in Osaka in 1941. He was a twin. His parents had designated Tadao as heir to his mother's family line and his maternal grandmother raised him. It is impossible to overstate Ando's grandmother's influence, exerted over the many years Tadao lived alone with her. Sometimes a father, then a mother, she became Tadao's most important mentor. Her character was suffused with the traditional rationalism and independence of an Osakan merchant family, and she instilled in her grandson a strict understanding of the essential rules of such a life. Ando had his tonsils removed as a child. On the morning of the operation, his grandmother handed him his washbowl, toothbrush and a change of clothes and sent the boy off to the hospital by himself. Although this shocked him, Ando now understands his grandmother's actions as a message to become a person sufficiently strong to overcome hardship alone. Thus Ando committed himself to self-reliance, no matter how demanding the circumstances. To survive alone one must be strong. The weak burden others. Ultimately, these principles lead to the conviction that even an individual has power to change the world.

For Ando, raised within Osaka's typical *shitamachi*, a mixed-use neighborhood comprising low-income row houses, shops and small factories, the streets served as school and the factories as classrooms. Every day, after school, Tadao frequented a carpenter's shop across the street from his grandmother's house. There he learned to recognize wood's personality and witnessed the precision of the human hand, which can work to an accuracy of 100th of one millimeter. He poured cast metal into a wooden frame of his own design, and blew glass at another nearby factory. Through these experiences, he developed a keen sensitivity to materials and now, when he formulates the details of a project, he starts from scratch, honing a knack for ideas that stem from the character and essence of each element, rather than from conventional designs. Tadao often visited a master carpenter who declared as he chiseled, "Even wood has character and you have to encourage it in the right direction." Craftsmanship requires perseverance but it also brings things nobly to life and offers the daily sense of accomplishment born of physical contact with its objects. An architect acquires freedom of imagination by removing himself from physical objects, but in doing so, loses his physical grounding. Ando still has a model boat that he made as a child. It bears witness to his respect for the master woodworker and his broader infatuation with craftsmen. Though he renounced the life of a craftsman to become an architect, his keen instincts for wood have survived. Ando's handmade cherry T-square and oak furniture are both immensely precise and clean. As one might expect, Ando has chosen dimensions that test the wood's limits.

Ando made his professional debut as a boxer at the age of 17, under the influence of his younger twin-brother, Takao Kitayama. Kitayama is a gifted commercial venue producer and has been a charismatic force in developing many of Japan's most fashionable venues. Although Ando also possesses a keen business sense, he chose to dedicate himself to solely to architecture. Together, he and his brother Kitayama have collaborated on many of Japan's cutting-edge commercial venues, including Kobe's Rose Garden, Takamatsu's Step, and Festival in Okinawa, but Ando has always focused exclusively on architecture.

Ando's boxing years bestowed many important life lessons. Though boxing is predicated on a battle between two individuals, it is also a private battle between body and soul. The boxer's will suppresses physical desires, quickening sensory reflexes and training the mind to make split-second judgments with unyielding determination. Boxing is a lonely and dangerous sport. Ando was to encounter the full scope of this on a solo tour of Thailand.

Through boxing, Ando relentlessly schooled himself in conquering fear, and to this day he maintains a boxer's self-discipline. He exercises for half an hour each night before bed. Starting with stretches, he exercises to strengthen his gums, his eyesight, his abdominal muscles, his back muscles and his upper arms. He has maintained this regimen every night for fifty years without a break. This personal ritual keeps his senses sharp, even as it rejuvenates him physically. It also manifests his essential philosophy that we achieve strength through continuity.

Since high school, Ando has walked the neighborhoods of Kyoto and Osaka exploring traditional Japanese homes and teahouses. It has been his method of education, allowing him to learn through physical rather than academic experience. These visceral journeys taught him a spatial sense of Japanese architecture. At 18, he earned his first design fee with a commission for a nightclub interior. This commission gave impetus for forays into furniture and interior design and his gradual movement towards architecture. He approached his work like a craftsman, using his hands to create, using his hands to think, in his own distinctive way. Later, he worked on redeveloping Kobe's Minatogawa District. The experience opened his eyes to city planning. As always, he approached his study of relationships between architectural endeavor, municipal regulations, socio-political systems, and economic enterprise with concrete practicality. He put this experience to work in later years, interpreting regulations, negotiating with bureaucrats and creating public works.

Ando longed for knowledge. But his nature was unsuited to the traditional school environment. Schools might offer knowledge, but their methods narrowed the breadth of his imagination commensurately. Ando believed that Japan's insipid academic system destroyed individuality. He never attended a university and never apprenticed himself to an established architect. He has had many mentors in life but none have been teachers of architecture. Self-taught, he has carved his own path in life. In the modern world, he is a singular architect. He possesses profound knowledge but it is drawn primarily from direct experience. He continues to collect and catalog books and routinely reads deep into the night, but he does not depend on books for his wisdom. For Ando, books serve as a catalyst for thought.

At 24, Ando left everything behind to travel the world. He was already a famous designer in Osaka and must have felt financially secure. Nonetheless, he decided to cast everything aside and start again. Abandoning his multiple careers as craftsman, boxer, interior designer, and city planner, he embarked on the path of architecture. His journey took him by boat from Yokohama to Nahodka where he caught the Trans-Siberian Railroad for Moscow, and then went on to Finland. After touring Europe's great cities, he boarded a ship at Marseilles bound for India via the Cape of Good Hope. Years later, Ando shared reminiscences of these travels with me.

Step, commercial complex, Takamatsu, Kagawa, 1977–1980

"Have you ever seen the horizon by sea and by land?" Recalling the distant horizon visible from Siberia's snowy steppes or from the Indian Ocean, Ando noted that the horizon is less an image than an experience. Travel on trains and ships gave him a visceral sense of the Earth. Intellectual knowledge is vastly different from concrete experience. He felt this keenly at the Ganges. People living vigorous lives in the heat, alongside death. The living perform ablutions in the Ganges and cremate their dead there. Life and death mingle in the heat. Earlier on his journey he resided in Finland's simple, clean architecture and soul purifying spaces, a world apart from India.

Ando speaks vividly of Impressionist paintings at the Hermitage, the flavor of a cup of coffee at Alvar Aalto's Rautatalo, and Heikki Siren's austere chapel with its exterior cross. Yet were these not odd obsessions for a young man during the 1960s? Ando had been involved with the Gutai Bijutsu Kyokai (Gutai Art Association), which aspired to the avant-garde in the late 1950s and '60s, and he had always preferred experimental art to traditional painting. Yet he valued Impressionist works against all expectation. His unbiased eye, stirred more deeply by Impressionism than Europe's cutting-edge avant-garde, is refreshing. It underscores the importance of dispensing with preconceptions in order to look with an honest eye, as well as the value of a critical perspective that permits self-analysis.

The simplicity and warmth of Finnish spaces suited Ando's temperament, but he recognized such architecture as a dangerous temptation and exhorted himself to strive for a more rigorous, if still less polished, aesthetic. As if to break out of his own shell, Ando continued to seek out not what he liked but whatever was most demanding. Later, when he traveled to America, he was deeply moved by the Shaker furniture and way of life. Ando's youthful journeys signal the start of his present life and remain his precious asset as an architect. He has since given extensive support to students studying abroad and has created a foundation that fosters international experience.

After a series of international journeys over nearly four years, Ando began life as an architect, opening his own office. A year later, he married Yumiko Kato. His first formal project was the Tomishima House. Originally commissioned by a personal friend, Ando eventually purchased it and has since used it for his office. He continually expands and renovates the structure, creating an ever-fascinating space. Truly a master of renovation, in life and in architecture, he is a wizard who transforms the coincidental into the inevitable.

With this office as his base, Ando involves himself in a variety of social activities. He frequently holds seminars, to which he invites philosophers, entrepreneurs and artists. In remembrance of those who died in the 1995 Kobe Earthquake, he established the Hyogo Green Network, which has planted 250,000 magnolia trees throughout the region. He also created Seto Inland Sea Olive Network Foundation, aimed at involving children in reviving habitats on the Inland Sea islands by planting olive and oak-trees. He often directs his gaze to children. When he walks along the streets, he listens to old people's stories and observes children in motion. Society's health can only be measured by the health of its children.

Ando has a rare talent for organizing and managing human networks and he continues to seek broader possibilities and responsibilities for the architect in society.

1969, at the age of 28 Ando established Tadao Ando Architect & Associates

The Geometry of Walls

Ando's architecture is an architecture of walls. For instance, a freestanding wall frames the natural surroundings as we approach the Church on the Water in Yufutsu, Hokkaido. In the Church of the Light in Osaka, an angled wall pierces a concrete cube. And in the Chichu Art Museum on Naoshima, a wall, bisected horizontally, encircles the inner courtyard like a medieval rampart. Ando has created many generous spaces through his experimental use of exposed concrete, but walls always play a crucial role.

Ando's works employ a limited range of materials and express their naked textures. His careful attention to materials gives his work its characteristic asceticism and tension. Ando's unadorned walls are powerful and heavy, even taciturn. The pristine materials crystallize their employer's intent. They cry out "Be pure, be beautiful, be strong," to those who behold them, who reside in them. The walls express an inner strength and in them we discover Ando's convictions.

Ando's early creations were concrete boxes. Mid-career, the walls of his structures grew brightly melodic. Ando's self-contained boxes gradually opened, admitting light, which poured in at the corners, illuminating the walls. His simple geometric formulas welcome nature and transformative light renders his spaces complex. He stages memorable architectural tableaux within external light by placing walls that slice the sky and reflect water.

Ando's inherent rhythm is upbeat and assertive, crisply articulate. Kidosaki House's white walls shimmer brightly, weaving a graceful melody that gently inflects the space. These are beautiful walls, brimming with gentle confidence.

Walls regulate movement and bring order to our lives. Walls guide us, impede us and govern our relationships. Walls command us, divide us, unite us, and bear responsibility and power over human relations. Nevertheless, Ando has managed to conceive walls which are gentle sanctuaries, replete with comfort and healing.

Ando does not divide space by function. Thus hard walls create malleable spaces. He preserves contiguous, ambiguous spaces allowing life latitude and gentleness.

Sketch for Kidosaki House, Setagaya-ku,
Tokyo, 1982–1986

At the same time, Ando's walls maintain a physicality which defy metaphor. Minimal-ist, they abjure sentimentality. His freestanding walls function like the planes of conceptual paintings, eliminating surface illusion, reducing the world to its essence. Beyond its visual beauty, Ando's architecture has the intensity of its naked materials. How does he himself view these materials?

"What I'm attempting to express through concrete is not Le Corbusier's rugged-ness but something more subtle." The touchstone for Ando's grasp of concrete lies in the rhythms of daily life, founded on Japan's unique aesthetics. From his earliest archi-tectural works, Ando has cherished materials with a unique intensity deeply tied to his childhood memories. Ando may be a master of poured concrete, but he relies on natural materials for points that a human being may touch. He inevitably uses natural wood for floors, doors, and furniture. As natural materials decay, they become reposi-tories for memory. God may well be in the details, but in Ando's architecture, mem-ories are in the details. Memory resides in the touch of things.

The Geometry of the Sky

Nature, especially the sky, plays a crucial role in Ando's architecture. He abstracts it to his purposes. "In order to elude architecture's fundamental nature as a closed-off box, I rely on the sky as the natural element which most affects architectural interiors." In Ando's architecture, the sky is a crucial spatial-structural element. When the sky breaks into song, an entire building sings. Whether designing a residence, a commercial prop-erty or an office building, Ando is always focused on how an entryway frames the sky. The interplay of light and shadow created by a sharply delineated sky and the three-dimensional forms expressed in concrete walls generate magnetism in Ando's archi-tecture. No other architect has ever been so concerned with the sky.

The sky is also a pivotal element in Ando's exterior spaces. He is skilled in bringing narrow and irregular sites to life. He is especially deft at utilizing irregular or sloping plots. His intuitive ability to read a site is phenomenal. In eliciting the latent power of a site, Ando weighs many factors, geographic orientation, sources of wind and light,

rainfall, runoff patterns, adjacent walls, the age of neighboring structures, and the flow of human traffic. Ando refers to his technique of treating an entire plot in three dimensions as "Site-craft." He models a three-dimensional sculpture out of thin air. Site-craft even renders blank space dimensionally. Through this process, the sky becomes the most vivid, closest aspect of nature. The blank space confined within a site speaks dynamically. Ando employs every last corner of a site. There is no dead space in his architecture.

Structure may dominate empty space but space can also dominate structure. The interlocking relationship between site, structure and empty space provides a formula for bringing a confined area to life. The structure requires an independent personality, but the blank space must have its own logic. Ando has applied this site-craft approach, a kind of three-dimensional interior-courtyard design, to housing complexes, and to commercial establishments. In his commercial properties, in particular, Ando creates a reversal effect between interior and exterior, resulting in structures with high efficiency ratios. Ando's ability to weave exterior and interior space transforms roads, courtyards, sky, and streetlights as it were into intimate interior spaces. In his open spaces one experiences the fullness of a rotunda that embraces a transparent ceiling.

In Ando's architecture, his central theme for exterior space is to render urban contexts architecturally. Ando incorporated Kobe's exotic Kitano-cho harbor context into Kitano Alley and Rose Garden. Kyoto's Time's floats quietly, like a ship on the banks of the Takase River, but a maze of complex alleys within the site evokes the streets of the ancient city. Sky and water, willow and wind join to create a depth of aerial perspective. It is the world of traditional Japanese painting.

The Aesthetics of Absence

Ando once called his Sumiyoshi Row House "The Provocative Box," and he articulates his architectural perspective in this way: "At first glance my architecture connotes exposure, as though I meant to create the kind of abstract space that results from stripping away all human, functional, and practical elements. In fact, I do not strive for abstract space but an archetype of space."

Ando's architecture is simple, strong and extremely gentle. It joins simplicity of form to complexity of space. It uses naked materials delicate to the touch. Above all, it conveys a clear image of life proposed by the simple form. This is critical. Clear geometry ushers in this simple image. Ando's architecture always contains a bold proposition for life or an element of incisive social criticism. His architectural philosophy flows in a steady line from his earliest works through the most recent. In this sense, Ando's architecture is not minimalist. It is true it relies on the unadorned box. But the unadorned wall arouses the imagination. It solicits the viewer's empathy precisely because it is unadorned.

Ando's concrete walls are suffused with elegant Japanese virtue and almost seem filled with sorrow. Bereft of apparent architectural elements, they stimulate the self-awareness of those who behold them, absorbing their gaze. Their polished concrete surfaces accept our empathy, like a Noh mask, and function almost as a mirror for our hearts. The walls reflect the patterns of our hearts, gradually absorbing our consciousness. The walls validate Ando's existence and engender his distinct aesthetic of absence. This is how they incite our imagination.

The mute walls reflect the landscape and the wind. As they reflect the air's invisible motion, the sound of the wind and the swaying of the trees seep into our hearts like shadow pictures. This effect, like a Japanese ink painting, at times generates a sense of the passing seasons or a *haiku*-like poetic effect. This, then, is the aesthetics of absence created by the silent walls. This is the reason why Ando's architecture is considered the culmination of Japanese aesthetics. Because the place of nothing is the essence of Japanese culture. A container for aesthetic emotions. A vessel for subjective empathy. Materials which are nothing in themselves generate abstract space because the lack of adornment invites a surfeit of empathy.

Although the Sumiyoshi Row House is a remarkable masterpiece of postwar residential history, on rainy days you need an umbrella to go to the toilet. The courtyard has no roof. That which belongs at the heart of the structure is missing. This is the greatest omission in this residence, and though normally forgotten, is a wound that throbs in the rain and wind and light. The greatest virtue of this house also resides in this wound. Because it goes without saying that the greatest theme of this residence is family love.

To love is to bestow what the other lacks. People love what is absent in them. Family love is formed around the roofless courtyard. The courtyard becomes the unconscious, invested with the memories of the community that is family. The light and the rain bring back the memories of life, stored in the geometry. The condition of lacking something which should be present stimulates the human spirit. It goes without saying that inviting nature into a dwelling makes life inconvenient. But there is something more precious than a convenient life. The Sumiyoshi Row House courtyard is an irreplaceable site in the life of the family.

Naked walls and a roofless courtyard. Ando's architecture, resolved to discard and unafraid of absence, is both the aesthetics of absence and an appeal that "Love is a function of absence."

Vitra seminar house, sketch

1975–1976 ▸ Row House
Sumiyoshi, Osaka

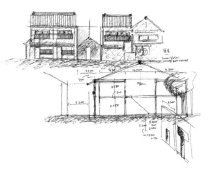

Row House, study drawing

Row House in Sumiyoshi is in Osaka's *shitamachi* ("low city") near Sumiyoshi Shrine. In the middle of this working class neighborhood full of the odors of everyday life stands a mute wall. Known as Osaka's "Deep South" district, this area is where Ando began his career. From the end of the 1960s to the early 1970s, Ando engaged in a struggle to create ample living spaces on narrow sites. It was a struggle to establish his identity as an architect while wrestling with complex factors—such as tradition and modernity, the desires and the limited budgets of clients, the exigencies of everyday life and the demands of aesthetics—in a city that still retains a strong Asian quality. Ando, who sees himself as a fighter-architect, developed a number of bold proposals for small houses. Among those houses, the Row House in Sumiyoshi is his crowning achievement—a fortress befitting an architect intent on developing his skills through repeated "trials of combat". It is also a house in which characteristics of his subsequent work are already evident.

Let us first take stock of the facts concerning the façade. We see an axially symmetrical composition, an overall form having a gatehouse-like character and a doorway in a central location. In the design of the elevation Ando uses only two rectangular forms: the overall outline of the building, and the doorway. From the drawings, we can also confirm that the entire site has been divided longitudinally into three parts and that the courtyard too has been divided into three equal parts. Tripartition is applied to the building as a whole and echoed by the rhythm of long-short-long on the façade, namely, wall-doorway-wall. Tripartition and axial symmetry are generally regarded as compositional rules of classical architecture. Although there are no columns here, many will probably judge this wall to be of the Doric or Tuscan order.

However, having a classical model does not fully explain the appeal of the Row House in Sumiyoshi. What makes this building appealing is the way a simple geometry produces an extremely rich spatial experience. Note, for example, the stairway in the courtyard. We turn left at the front entrance, enter the courtyard, turn 180 degrees to ascend the stairway, turn 180 degrees once more, cross the bridge and arrive at a bedroom at the far end of the second floor. A complex circulation plan transforms a simple geometry into a rich spatial experience. That is Ando's spatial magic at work. This progression—a clear geometry followed by a complex circulation plan leading to a rich spatial experience—is a technique for transforming through experience a cold geometrical schema into a place of life, and is fundamental to Ando's architecture.

Ando's treatment of nature in the city is something else that distinguishes his work. The courtyard of the Row House in Sumiyoshi is a secluded space cut off from the commotion of the city; it is open only to the sky. The courtyard is a window, accepting light, wind and rain so that nature is able to seep into the spirit of the observer. When we stand in the courtyard and look up at the stars in the night sky, the mute walls frame the landscape and we are made aware of the flow of air and intimations of the changing seasons. That is because the courtyard, made of concrete, glass, and slate, reflects incident light and causes complex shadows. This is the moment when Ando's

Left page:
Street façade
The concrete box contrasts sharply with the neighborhood landscape.

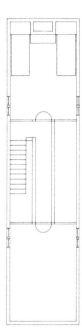

mute walls create a poetic, *haiku*-like effect. (*Haiku* is a highly concise, traditional form of Japanese poetry, often having a seasonal theme.) For the family the space becomes much larger than its mere physical extent. It becomes a world in miniature. Matter has a psychological effect on the observer precisely because the absence of ornament invites extraordinary empathy. That is the reason why Ando's buildings are said to be the ultimate expression of the Japanese sense of beauty. A place of nothingness is in the very nature of Japanese culture.

The Row House in Sumiyoshi has a social theme as well as a design theme. Ando introduces a concrete box amidst the dilapidated wooden row houses that crowd the central areas of Osaka and creates a highly self-sufficient living space inside that box. Ando ensures individual privacy, something traditional townhouses were unable to provide; he creates a residential space that enables modern individuals to develop. For Ando, architecture can be a weapon for social reform. Ando agonized over the question "architecture or revolution?" in his twenties but eventually chose architecture. He became convinced that "to change the dwelling is to change the city and to reform society." Row House in Sumiyoshi is an expression of Ando's belief that the house is precisely the building type that can change society.

With its simple composition and variegated spaces, its sense of closure, and its living spaces dramatized by light, the Row House in Sumiyoshi is the architectural prototype of Ando's imagination.

since 1978 ‣ Rokko Housing I, II, III, IV

Kobe, Hyogo

Building site, Rokko Housing I

Left page:
Aerial view of the complex

Plan of Rokko Housing I, II and III

The site is a south-facing hillside with a 60-degree slope in the foothills of the Rokko Mountains in Kobe. Ando took on the challenge offered by the site with great determination. This complex, which clings to the side of a hill like a rock-climber, is unique in appearance. The project was risky from the standpoint of technology, laws and regulations, and economics. The building could not have been designed by anyone other than Ando. Shown the original hillside, who else would have had the madcap idea of constructing an apartment building on this incline after they had seen it?

The first phase was begun in 1978 and completed in 1983. Two years after its completion, Ando published the second phase for an apartment complex four times the size of the first phase. After nearly eight years, the second phase was completed, whereupon he immediately embarked on a third. That was completed in 1999. Today, a fourth phase is in progress. Ando has continued building in this area for 30 years, as if determined to cover the entire hillside with his buildings. He has overseen the development of this cluster of apartment buildings in great detail, even taking the time to occasionally water plants himself. He has a unit of his own here.

The first-phase complex is a three-dimensional grid, based on a unit 5.4 meters by 4.8 meters in plan, following the slope. The 20 apartment units step back on the hillside, using the roofs of lower levels as terraces; the result is a cluster of independent units, each with its own character. Greenery penetrates the interiors of the building, enabling the occupants to lead lives at one with nature. The idea of the roof terrace has often been used in subsequent projects by Ando.

The second-phase complex is next to the first phase, but the two projects are independent of one another. A square module, 17 feet by 17 feet in plan, was used in the second phase; the vertical overlapping of square grids has created unexpected views. Three-dimensional geometrical arrangements help establish straightforward, uninhibited relationships between residents and between residents and nature.

Three types of gardens are provided in order to generate various communal relationships: the terraces that serve as the front gardens of individual units; a middle courtyard that serves as a plaza where people gather; and the rear garden, a stroll path where seasonal flowers bloom in profusion. These three gardens are respectively private, communal and public in nature. They are places for different types of communication that can enliven everyday life: the terrace provides a view of the harbor and a nightscape of Kobe; the middle courtyard is a place for a brief chat among neighbors; the path is a place where a resident can stroll alone to appreciate the effects of the changing season on the landscape.

The third phase is a large project, approximately seven times the size of the second phase. Here, Ando sought to lower the cost by introducing prefabrication. Besides low-rise buildings with courtyards, there are, for the first time, high-rise buildings. As in the earlier two phases, the spaces between buildings are designed as common spaces, but in the third phase, the stepped path in the north-south direction following the slope of the site and green areas that extend in the east-west direction crisscross in plazas. The

Open community space. Rokko Housing II

common spaces are highly nuanced and remind one of the Halen Housing Project (1955–1961) near Bern, Switzerland, by Atelier 5.

The three phases are actually three development projects for different clients on different sites, carried out at different times. Ando's ability to endow the three projects with a harmonious, continuous townscape commands admiration.

He has analyzed the relationship between individual elements and the group, and has translated the principles for combining units in a housing complex into clear rules of spatial composition. People can face each other, look out in the same direction or stand back to back. It should be noted that the prototypes for these forms of spatial organization, based on human relationships, correspond to the Row House in Sumi-yoshi, the Koshino House and the Kidosaki House. Ando is a diligent student; in his youth he did research to see how the neighborhood-unit theory or the idea of the *Unité d'habitation* could be adopted in Japan. The Kingohusene Housing Project (1957–1960) near Helsingør by Jørn Utzon and Søholm Terraced Housing (1950) near Copenhagen by Arne Jacobsen are among his favorite residential projects.

To get from the individual element to the group, Ando begins by establishing the individual element, then translates into space the relationship between individual elements to organize a larger group form. Rokko Housing is a space that has been logic-ally developed on the basis of rules of combination. Moreover, three factors—rules of spatial organization that apply to the entire complex, highly individualistic interior spaces, and shared spaces that make full use of the advantages of being a group—give rise to the ambience of a quiet, high-class residential district.

Left page:
Rokko Housing II
Banks of stairways allow each level to be reached
on foot from the exterior.

1979–1980, 1983–1984 ▸ Koshino House

and Annex ▸ Ashiya, Hyogo

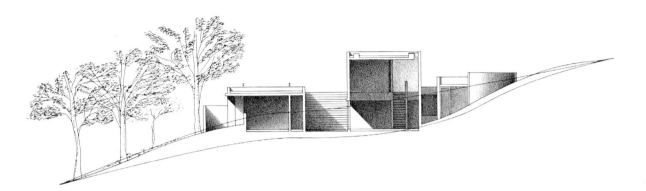

Section drawing, geometrical figures in the gentle slope

Left page:
Two boxes and a segmented cylinder are set in the woods.

The Koshino House represented a fresh start for Ando. He began the work of dismantling the architectural prototype developed earlier in the Row House in Sumiyoshi and of reassembling the pieces. He gradually opened up the closed box, allowed interior and exterior spaces to communicate through gaps in the walls and between walls and the roof, and organized carefully worked-out spaces. The expressive themes became the fine texture of walls and dramatization by means of light; he began to use topography even more flexibly in organizing space. Ando calls the act of designing a site "site-craft"; he blends together the site and the building, incorporates the landscape into the building, and makes use of every bit of the site. The interior space is extended into the exterior space, and the entire site is transformed into a space as precisely assembled as craftwork.

For Ando, a closed box is the prototype for houses on small sites in central Osaka. However, the Koshino House is located on a hillside in a lush natural environment. It is a concrete building, beautiful and relaxed in the midst of nature. The corners of the box, hitherto firmly closed, have been loosened, bit by bit. Light enters through a skylight between the wall and the roof, illuminating a curved wall; a large window has been opened in the living room wall. The interior is gradually assimilated into the beautiful landscape.

This house is composed of two box-like buildings of different volumes, arranged in parallel on either side of a terrace. The main building contains a double-height living room, a kitchen, a dining room, and, on an upper floor, the main bedroom. The other building is the private quarters, accommodating a total of six rooms—bedrooms and *tatami* rooms—arranged in a row, as well as a bathroom. The two buildings are connected by an underground corridor. Then there is the terrace between the two buildings—an outdoor living room where one can fully appreciate the abundant greenery. Ando suggests a life in which the occupant is made continually aware of the richness of nature on a spacious site surrounded by trees. This building, which can be used to accommodate guests on weekends, is predicated on a lifestyle very different from that in the city.

An atelier was added four years after the completion of the house. Ando's buildings are always formally complete. Thus, his task is additionally to alter a form that was once complete in itself to create another complete form. The end result must rise to a new level of perfection. Adding a few touches to a work completed in the past is difficult.

In the case of the Koshino House, Ando sought to develop a new overall image by contrasting the addition to the existing portion. The addition is positioned higher up on the hillside; a wall describing a quadrant in plan resists soil pressure like a dam and encloses a space. A slit is opened in the ceiling along the curving wall of the addition, and light entering through the slit takes the form of a curving geometrical figure. This is in strong contrast to the existing portion, where light from the skylight takes a linear form; the two parts of the house offer different spatial experiences even at the same time of day. The addition was not anticipated at the beginning, but Ando has succeeded in forming a landscape of even greater complexity and nuance.

Ando is a master of additions and renovations. He is always assimilating images and picturing possible worlds so that, if the slightest opportunity presents itself, he can immediately try to realize them. In 2005, he is in fact in the process of a second

View into the living/dining area

Right page above:
The living room: sharp contrasts between light and shade

Right page below:
Hallway outside the bedrooms

renovation of the Koshino House. Twenty-five years after the completion of the original residence in 1980, he is at work on a new project. His versatility—his ability to use a wide range of imagery—makes possible flexible additions. This ability has served him well in projects to preserve buildings. That is because projects to construct new facilities while preserving old buildings do indeed need to transcend time.

1982–1986 ▸ Kidosaki House
Setagaya-ku, Tokyo

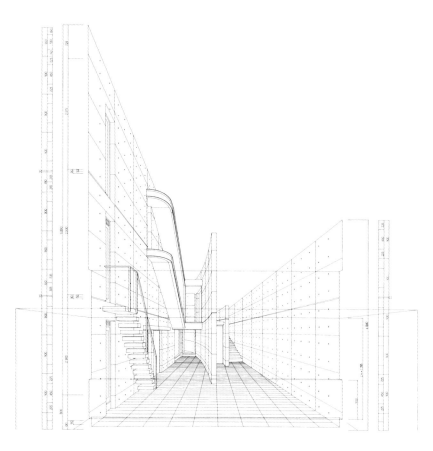

Perspective drawing of the inner courtyard

Left page:
View into the lower level living room

The Kidosaki House is a house of great refinement located in a quiet residential district not far from the center of Tokyo. Its spaces are breathtaking in their sheer beauty. There is little for this writer to comment on with respect to this work. The beauty of its spaces leaves the observer at a loss for words. There is a sense of ease and elegance about the house. That is because we have a feeling here of time and life spent in leisure. The house can be tiny or spacious, the client affluent or not so affluent – Ando never changes his approach. He always discovers a theme unique to that house and invents something original that makes everyday life more enjoyable. In the case of the Kidosaki House, that something was elegant beauty. White is used in the interior spaces, in response in part to a request by the client's mother. This whiteness endows the spaces with splendor and radiance.

This is a three-household house, for a husband and wife and their respective parents. The program called for a design that would enable the three families to live together but preserve the privacy of each household. Courtyards were the key. The three-story building is based on a 20 foot-square grid. The intention was to create complex spaces

within a simple composition. This large residence is in marked contrast to the Row House in Sumiyoshi, but is an extension of the earlier work in the sense that space is developed around a courtyard. Ando takes the idea of the courtyard from the traditional townhouses of Japan but, using concrete, develops multi-level courtyards, something that cannot be achieved in wooden architecture. These courtyards are spaces for introducing nature into the three households and assuring those households their privacy.

The rooms look out onto courtyards, but diverse windows—such as low windows and full-height windows—are used in combination so that persons in different rooms never find themselves looking directly at each other. Ando arranges the windows symmetrically and clearly establishes frontality; he also takes ventilation into consideration in designing the sash. With double sliding windows, he uses concealed stiles to solve the problem of both design and function.

The same varieties of plants that once grew on the site have been planted in the front courtyard on the north side and the south courtyard. This is intended to preserve the history of the site and links with the past in the minds of those living here, even though the house itself has been rebuilt. The trees, together with the vines and shrubs planted in the scattered gardens and terraces, create a landscape responsive to the seasons and provide a dramatic backdrop to everyday life.

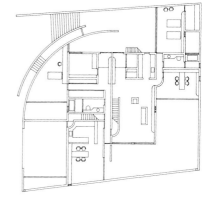

Above:
The living room on the main floor

Below:
Plan of the first floor

The client, Hirotaka Kidosaki, is himself an architect whose works have been awarded many prizes. Why then did he commission Ando instead of designing the house himself? In an interview, Kidosaki answered as follows. "There would have been a reluctance to speak out and conflicts of interest had I tried designing a house for my relations. Instead, as the person in charge on the client side, I concentrated on being a coordinator and producer, clarifying the wishes of relatives and communicating them to the architect."

Kidosaki sees his own house with the cool detachment of a professional. A surgeon, no matter how skilled, would never operate on himself. Kidosaki introduced an outsider, that is, Ando, precisely because it was a house for himself and his relatives. The move was insightful.

Ando so far has not designed a detached house for himself. Designing a house for another architect is a curious and interesting problem.

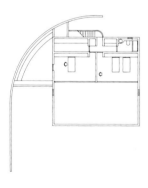

Above:
Exterior view

Below:
Plan of the third floor

1985–1988 ‣ Church on the Water
Yufutsu, Hokkaido

Exterior view

Church on the Water stands in the midst of Hokkaido's magnificent natural environment. Hokkaido, a region of cold winters, is located at the northern end of the Japanese archipelago. The surrounding area is thickly wooded. From spring through summer, it is covered with greenery. The leaves turn brown in autumn, and the region is covered with snow in winter. The church is a place in this rich natural environment where we can hear the blowing of the wind, the murmur of a stream and the songs of birds.

A natural brook has been diverted to form an artificial lake, and the church, which has a geometrical form, stands against the background of the lake. This landscape, integrating natural scenery, garden and architecture, is a masterpiece of contemporary Japanese landscape design. The landscape gardens of England, the geometrical gardens of continental Europe, the famous gardens of China and the gardens of Islam are well known, but examples in contemporary architecture of the reconstruction of a natural landscape on such a grand scale are rare.

A wall, L-shaped in plan, shields the building proper and the artificial lake, and guides us to the church. At first, the water is hidden from sight by the extended wall. As we walk, we hear only the sound of the water. Turning the corner at one end of the wall, we suddenly see the wide expanse of the lake. There is a sense of release, as if our bodies were melting into the landscape.

The building plan is two overlapping squares, one 50 feet to a side and the other 33 feet. In the smaller square, four crosses are arranged with their ends nearly touching.

View into the landscape
The cross stands alone in the lake.

The walls are double-layered for heat insulation because of the cold winters. The total thickness of the exposed concrete walls, both outside and inside the building, is 35 inches, which includes a middle layer of styrofoam. The floor too is double-layered, and all rooms have underfloor heating. The technical measures and the detailing throughout the building must have required great effort to devise and execute, but no trace of that effort is apparent on the surface. The harsh environment has given birth to a beautiful landscape, and effort not apparent to observers has given birth to a beautiful building. Seemingly effortless effort has created a crystalline space.

Ando has designed three churches: Chapel on Mt. Rokko (referred to in Japan as Church of the Wind) halfway up a mountain near Kobe, Church of the Light in a residential district in an Osaka suburb, and Church on the Water in the grand natural environment of Hokkaido. These buildings are designed around three natural elements—wind, light and water. Although Ando uses concrete in all three churches, they are very different buildings; each has its own unique character. He in fact has an idea for a church of the sea—a church washed by the waves. Just the idea of it is highly evocative. Ando is always able to explain his work concisely and to captivate a listener immediately.

1987–1989 ▸ Church of the Light

Ibaraki, Osaka

The church in the suburban environment of Ibaraki City

This building was built with donations from members of the church. The budget was 25 million yen (about US$ 218.000). At first, Ando believed there was not enough money to complete the building. There might be enough to put up the walls but not to roof the church. He therefore imagined that there would be initially an open-air chapel, with the walls framing the sky. The roof could be put up if enough donations were collected in four or five years' time. Creating a building gradually might be an interesting process.

In fact, the building was completed thanks to the enthusiasm of the members of the church and the construction company. Even in contemporary times, buildings are realized not just for economic reasons, but through enthusiasm and religious faith. This was an emotionally moving experience for Ando.

The building is box-shaped and large enough to inscribe three spheres 19 feet in diameter; the box is penetrated by a wall at a 15-degree angle. The diagonal wall, which is completely freestanding, divides the main space into the chapel and a vestibule. From the vestibule, we pass through an opening in the diagonal wall and, turning 180 degrees, find ourselves in the chapel. A cruciform slit in the wall at the far end of the chapel is bathed by the morning sun, creating a cross of light. The church is like the inside of a pinhole camera; the cross of light is dazzling.

Light is the theme of this building, but at the same time, creating darkness was important because light becomes radiant only against the backdrop of a profound darkness. Here, nature is rendered extremely abstract; it is limited only to light. Architectural space is purified.

The floor and the benches are made of rough wood planks normally used for scaffolding. Although this was made necessary by the limited budget, it has a positive effect in that we are made directly aware of the texture of the material. Ando is critical of the present tendency to eliminate materiality in architecture and to use characterless, artificial materials in the name of economic rationalism. He always uses natural materials for parts of the building with which people come into physical contact. He believes that materials of substance such as wood, stone and concrete are important for architecture, and that they enable us to sense the building directly through our bodies.

The church offers both representational nature and abstract nature. A rectilinear patch of light is cast on the floor; natural materials that appeal to the senses are left in darkness. Our spirits soar. Through light too, we are made to recognize in the most basic sense our relationship to nature.

Noboru Karukome, the minister of the church, is deeply satisfied with the building. "A Protestant church is simple to begin with. There is little ornament. However, if that is taken too far, you end up with just a meeting hall. Ando did a magnificent job of creating a 'church'. I think he created a truly rich space."

Ten years later, a Sunday school was added to the Church of the Light. The school is not a place of prayer but instead a facility equipped with a hall, a library and a kitchen to support activities by members of the church. From the outside, the Sunday school

Left page:
Interior of the church with cruciform opening

Right:
Exterior view of cruciform

Below:
Study of the angles at which light will enter the interior space

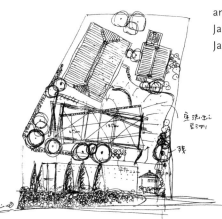

and the church are a matched pair of forms, but inside, the school is finished in Japanese linden; the built-in furniture, too, is made of plywood boards faced with Japanese linden. The space is simple yet brightly illuminated.

1988–1995 · Naoshima Contemporary Art Museum

Benesse House and Annex ▸ Naoshima, Kagawa

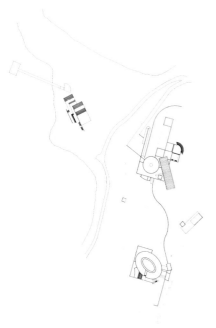

Naoshima Contemporary Art Museum stands on a promontory on a small island floating in the Inland Sea. The building is relaxed and at rest—stretched out as if to enjoy the view of the sea. The spacious site creates an impression of brightness, lightness and outward orientation; curved lines seem to dance joyously. The inward-oriented seriousness of Ando's works in cities is absent; instead there is a sense of release about this building. Eluding geometry of an inhibiting, prescriptive character, the building has seemingly fled to nature in search of freedom and release. We sense a centrifugal force at work. Walls of natural stone, terraces, and plazas are arranged throughout the site. Here, nature and architecture disport themselves; climate and geometry melt into one another.

Let us approach this museum by boat from the sea. Like the entrance to a house, the pier welcomes us. Next, there is a concrete wall and a broad terraced plaza of natural stone. This is a garden placed in the midst of maternal nature, a device that articulates and draws attention to the latter. Ando creates a landscape out of nature with minimal manipulation. That was always the traditional predisposition of Japanese culture. For example, correlations between Ando's spaces and Japanese *haiku* have been pointed out from time to time. *Haiku* is an extremely short verse form of a highly normative character; it must contain a "season word" and three metrical units of five, seven, and five syllables respectively. Using geometry, Ando likewise articulates the landscape into phrases and generates another nature within nature.

Plan of the original structures and phase II on the right

Right:
An oval pond fills the center of the building of the phase II.
The shape of the sky and the shape of the pond correspond to one another.

Left page:
The beautiful and traditional landscape in Setonaikai national park

Let us look at his plans. A hotel, an art museum, a restaurant, and a hall are arranged radially around an enormous cylinder. Function and geometry are clearly coordinated. The radial composition of space projects an image of centrifugal force. However, it is impossible to get an overall image of the building from any angle because the building is embedded in the ground. We can experience only a portion of the space at any one time. Our eyes shift from one direction to another in search of an overall image.

The cylinder, on the other hand, is a node integrating vertical lines of circulation. However, because of the sloping topography, we are underground in one room but find ourselves above ground in the next. As we move, the landscape blends into the geometry; nature and geometry are at play. The landscape breaks through the perimeter of the building and invades the interior; the rooms are filled, each with a different landscape.

Two very large granite spheres by Walter de Maria. Installed in a covered space below the main buildings and above the boat dock.

Upon completion of the museum, a second phase consisting mainly of lodgings was built on a hill behind the museum. A cable car takes us from the museum to the top of the hill. Leaving behind the station, we pass through a garden with a waterfall; we see a water garden at the bottom of an elliptical opening in the hill. The water reflects the sky framed by the ellipse. The guest rooms arranged around the elliptical garden afford beautiful views of the Inland Sea. This is a "detached palace" in a quiet world of its own.

Light and air, rendered extremely abstract, fill the interior spaces of Ando's religious buildings and private houses. In this work, however, the landscape is quite specific. By enabling us to actually "feel" specific objects and phenomena in the landscape such as sunsets, the wake of a boat, cresting waves, silhouettes of distant islands and stormy skies, he creates spaces that restore to us our physicality and sensitivity.

Interior view with circular ramp

Right:
**Sketch showing the steep topography
of the site**

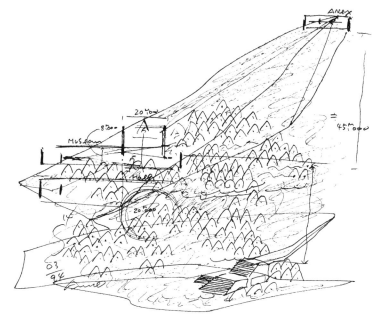

1989–1991▸Water Temple Hompuku-ji

Tsuna, Hyogo

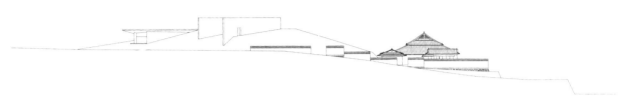

Elevation showing the insertion of the new temple into the natural topography of the hillside

Left page:
The two outer walls and the floating pond

Look at this photograph of a priest descending into a lotus pond. This was Ando's architectural solution to the problem of making manifest in this world the Paradise of Buddhist teaching. He imagined a person crossing a lotus pond and a hall appearing up ahead. The symbolism and image are dynamic. We can almost imagine paradise to be such a place. The question was creating a space that enables visitors to have such an experience.

Water Temple is located on top of a hill at the northeastern part of Awaji Island, which affords a view of Osaka Bay. It is the main hall of Hompuku-ji, a temple belonging to the Ninna-ji branch of the Shingon sect. In Buddhism, the lotus symbolizes the attainment of enlightenment by Shaka (Sanskrit: Sakyamuni). This temple embodies Ando's wish to create a hall where Buddha and all living things might sleep, wrapped in a lotus. Intense images experienced in India in his youth are burned into Ando's memory. A monkey riding on the back of a horse, and a bird perched on the head of the monkey. This is a world where human beings, animals, and nature coexist, all distinctions having been swept away—a space where life and death, the sacred and the profane, form a harmonious whole.

First, he set an elliptical lotus pond, with a major axis of 130 feet and a minor axis of 98 feet, on top of the hill. Next, he cut open the pond in the middle and placed a stairway leading down. We descend the stairway as if we were sinking and disappearing into the bottom of the pond and come upon a vermilion-colored, otherworldly hall. The hall consists of a round room with a diameter of 46 feet placed inside a room 57 feet by 57 feet in plan. The round room is divided by regularly-spaced columns with a square cross-section and a lattice screen into the outer sanctuary and the inner sanctuary. This re-creates an ancient spatial arrangement conforming to Shingon-sect ritual. The succession of geometrical spaces—ellipse, square, circle and grid—heightens our concentration as we gradually approach the most sacred area. The elliptical lotus pond and the vermilion hall underneath the pond are joined by a highly dramatic path of circumambulation.

Let us consider the spatial experience leading up to arrival at the hall. Climbing a path covered with white sand and surrounded by greenery, we see a straight wall. This wall clearly divides the blue sea and the sky and provides a frame of reference for the landscape. Once we are past this wall, a gently curving wall leads us deeper into the

Monks stepping down the stairs bisecting the lotus pond

space. The path of white sand flanked by straight and curved walls is a domain mediating between the everyday world and the sacred world. The path of white sand underneath the blue sky framed by the walls is dazzling. We follow the curving wall to its end and turn the corner; suddenly the lotus pond appears in front of us. After the sea and the sky comes the lotus pond. As we experience dissimilar spaces, our sense of expectation increases. We wonder what will appear next. It is with a sense of exultation that we are swallowed by the water in the middle of the lotus pond. Water Temple is truly an attempt to express in time and space the dramatic transition from the everyday world to the realm of the sacred. When the rays of the setting sun enter through the western window of the underground hall, the vermilion space becomes brilliantly red; a space is revealed that transcends the everyday world.

Ando himself has explained his thoughts about this building in the following way. "The concrete will weather and trees will encroach on the pond as time passes. However, in summer, the lotus blossoms will still flower and remind people that this place is sacred. Contemporary architecture is concerned only with the present; buildings compete for momentary splendor. I would like to create buildings that continue to live on, however much they change in appearance."

1989–1992 ▸ Japan Pavilion
Expo '92 ▸ Seville, Spain

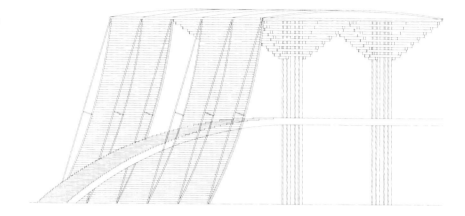

Ando designed the Japan Pavilion for the 1992 International Exposition in Seville, Spain. The pavilion is an enormous wooden building. The aim of the pavilion was to acquaint people in the rest of the world with the traditional aesthetic of Japan, an aesthetic based on unadorned simplicity. The mission of this project was to reinterpret wood architecture with leading-edge contemporary technology and create a building that embodied tradition and modernity, technology and culture. Ando usually tries to create spaces that communicate the Japanese spiritual character, using modern materials such as concrete, steel and glass.

Here, however, he had a different objective: to reinterpret the technology of Japanese wood architecture by means of contemporary technology. The curved exterior walls of laminated lap siding evoke Japanese tradition. However, Ando had no intention of forcing traditional Japanese culture on visitors; the roof is made of Teflon-coated fabric. This pavilion was constructed with materials, skills and workmen gathered from the United States, Europe and Africa. The exchange of art, information and technology was an important element of the project; it was from that exchange that this building was born.

Plan of the first floor

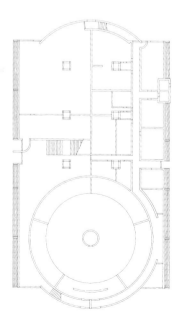

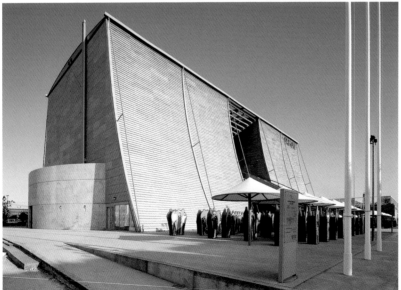

Exterior view through the access area

Left:
View from southwest

View above the access ramp

Right:
The access area

1998–2000 ▸ Komyo-ji Temple
Saijo, Ehime

The Temple to the left and the old bell tower
The walkway is curved to make way for this remnant of the previous temple complex.

Komyo-ji is a temple in a small town called Saijo, Ehime Prefecture, on the island of Shikoku. This town is blessed with abundant spring water, and is covered with a network of clean canals. The project called for rebuilding a dilapidated main hall together with the guest hall and the priests' living quarters. For such a small temple, this was a major, historic project. The abbot made no specific requests concerning the architecture. He only stated a wish to create "a temple to which people would come, a temple that was open to the community."

Ando proposed "a wooden hall wrapped in a soft light and floating on water." The wooden main hall floating on a pond of spring water is a space made of water, a basic element in the landscape of the region, and wood, a material that evokes the mountains of Shikoku.

Ando believes that the *nandaimon* (great south gate) of Todaiji and the Jodo Hall of Jodoji, both designed by the abbot Chogen (1121–1206), contain the essence of traditional Japanese wood architecture. Both buildings have been designated National Treasures and are extant examples of the *daibutsu* (or *tenjiku*) style of construction. The bracket system is what makes the style distinctive. The brackets transmit the weight of the roof to the columns. Ando believes that a powerful structural aesthetic is the starting point for wood construction; the role played by each member and the way force is transmitted from one member to the next should be clear to the observer. In other words, he believes a building should make manifest, simply and honestly, the flow of forces. For Ando, this is more than simple structural expressionism; the structure is symbolic of the way people come together and through cooperation form a community.

Left page:
The wooden structure of the temple is separated by water from the concrete building where the burial area is located.

The space of the main hall is a room equivalent to 100 *tatami* mats in size. Four sets of four pillars, or 16 pillars in all, arranged at the four corners of the space support three layers of beams. The main hall is wrapped in a double-layered envelope of frosted glass and lattices. That is, the main hall is wrapped in frosted glass and surrounded by a corridor, on the outside of which are lattices fitted with glass. Sunlight passes through the lattices and the corridor, and, filtered by the frosted glass, fills the entire main hall with a soft, uniform light. The view at night is also beautiful. At night, the situation is reversed; light from the main hall is scattered and reflected by the pond, creating a visionary atmosphere.

However, the technology used in this building is different from that of traditional Japanese wood architecture. The wooden members are not solid wood but laminated wood. Perhaps Ando chose laminated wood because the quality of the material is uniform; laminated timber can be fully used, from end to end, with no waste. Or perhaps he used it because the way layers of wood are glued together to form one member is

Right page below:
The light-filled walkway that surrounds the main temple space

symbolically apt for a temple supported by a group of people. In this temple project, Ando's approach was realistic and gentle, flexible and pliant. In creating the building, he accepted the memory of the place, read the context of the site, and took advantage of the balmy climate.

1990–1994▸Chikatsu-Asuka Historical Museum

Minamikawachi, Osaka

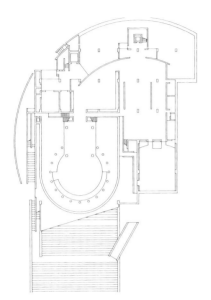

Plan of the basement

Drawing of the step roof with tower

This building is bold and architectural ambition is embodied in a brilliantly simple design. Architectural ambition is the will to give order to the world, not through language or metaphysics, but design. As for this work, the reckless attempt to divide the world into two realms by means of an enormous stone stairway is nothing less than architectural ambition.

The roof of the museum is a low-pitched stairway paved with several hundred thousand pieces of white granite; from the stairway three ashen concrete towers rise toward the sky. The stairway suggests to us Greek ruins or the Pyramids. Most of all, we are made to realize once more how bright and free a stairway toward the sky can be. It is a pure, intellectual space composed through geometry. Beyond the topmost step, like a lace curtain, are the treetops of the forest of Chikatsu-Asuka, continuing upward toward the heavens. The white stone podium is a threshold to infinite space. The realm above the stairway is a place of reason, of what the Greeks called *idea*, that is, forms or patterns.

Below the stairway lies the realm of passions. It is a museum dedicated to *kofun* (burial mounds), and at the same time, a space where ancient spirits dwell, the dwelling place of the *genius loci*. It is not so much a gallery space as an underground theater teeming with emotions flitting hither and thither. Thus, the enormous stone stairway forms a boundary between opposing realms: light and darkness; centrifugal force and centripetal force; intellect and emotions; history and archaeology; museum and tomb.

Still, this building is a dangerous work that cannot be completely explained in terms of the opposition of macrocosm versus microcosm—it is a building like no other. There is no other building in the world in which a stairway plays such an important role.

What Ando's buildings always communicate to us is the conviction that architecture is able to give order to the world only when it is based on strong emotions, and

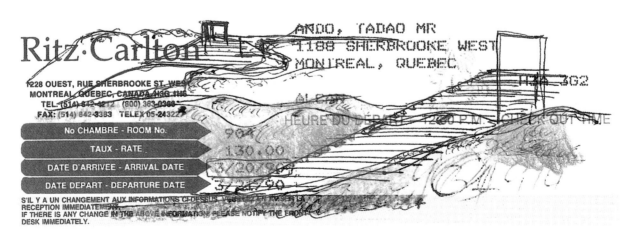

Aerial view of the step roof that also functions as an open theater

the faith that strong emotions are born only by taking up challenges and prevailing. Beauty is not the goal of architecture, only the result.

The area of the site in southern Osaka Prefecture is known for its many burial mounds; well over 200 mounds including four imperial mausolea and the tombs of famous historical figures such as the statesman Prince Shotoku (574–622) and the diplomat Ono no Imoko (circa early 7th century) are scattered over the area. It is an environment in which we can sense the long flow of time from the dawn of Japanese history to the present. This building is a facility dedicated to the display and research of *kofun* culture, but it has also been conceived as a hill that affords a panoramic view of the surrounding burial mounds. The stepped roof is an observation deck, plaza, open-air theater and undulating artificial hill.

1991–1994 · Museum of Wood
Mikata, Hyogo

Exterior view of the museum with its long approach walkway

Inside view with the spiral walkway

Left page:
Contrasts between circle and axis in the forest

Ando designed a facility called the Museum of Wood in 1994 in a mountainous area of Hyogo Prefecture in Japan. This is a museum that provides an introduction to wood cultures around the world. The task was to create a place that enables visitors to experience a culture of wood through the senses; Ando's solution was to construct a powerful wooden frame on a wooded mountainside—a structure designed to be embedded in the environment. The buildings that best express the Japanese attitude and approach to wood are Shinto shrines, Buddhist temples, *machiya* (traditional townhouses) and teahouses, but the Museum of Wood is an entirely different building type.

The building encloses a tall, ring-shaped space, 150 feet in diameter and 52.5 feet in ceiling height. A veritable forest of laminated pillars and crisscrossed beams fills the space. The center of the ring is a circular pond open to the sky. Thus a space of sky and water, enclosed by a ring-shaped space constructed of wood, has been inserted into the woods. We pass through a thickly wooded natural forest, encounter a powerful wooden structure, and arrive at the void of sky and water at its center.

A wooden structure with such a clear geometrical space is highly unusual. The building seems to have a primitive, magical force; at the same time, it suggests a structure from some distant future out of a science-fiction novel or a sort of wooden pyramid.

Ando makes highly precise wooden furniture. As for architecture, he is not content to remain within the realm of traditional Japanese architecture but has taken on projects that expand the possibilities of wooden construction.

1991–2001 ▸ Pulitzer Foundation for the Arts
St. Louis, Missouri, USA

The sketch of the Foundation shows the double rectangle.

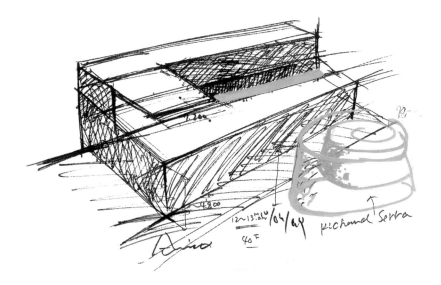

This art museum was commissioned by Joseph Pulitzer Jr., the grandson of Joseph Pulitzer, the newspaper publisher known throughout the world for the prizes awarded in his name. It houses the art collection of the Pulitzer family. The site is in St. Louis, Missouri, which is located in the American Midwest at the confluence of the Mississippi and the Missouri Rivers. St. Louis developed as the gateway to the West in pioneer days and has an illustrious history. However, by 1991 the city was troubled by sprawl and the decay of the central district. At first, this development was intended to be a key part of a project to revive culture in St. Louis; the idea was to convert an old automobile factory in the city into an art museum.

The illness and death of Joseph Pulitzer during the phase of studying the factory and the preparation of a scheme forced the project back to square one. It was decided that an entirely new concept would be developed; the project began with the selection of a site together with Emily Rauh Pulitzer, who had taken over the direction of her late husband's project.

From the start, artists such as Richard Serra and Ellsworth Kelly participated in the project as advisors; the project proceeded as a collaboration between the architect and artists. Naturally, the artists sought galleries that would show their works to the greatest advantage. Ando tried to create introspective spaces suitable for a dialogue with art. Collaboration with individuals of uncompromising artistic temperaments was extremely tense work. Conflicts arose between the strong personalities involved. Mrs. Pulitzer, too, was an expert, with considerable experience as a museum curator, and progress would have been impossible without her understanding. The tumultuous dialogue between architect and artists lasted ten years. The museum was at last completed in October 2001.

Left page:
The main gallery
Art work by Ellsworth Kelly of honeycomb aluminum which was commissioned by the Pulitzer Foundation and placed here for symbiosis with the architecture.

Exterior view
The free-standing wall and the concrete box are
a typical configuration of Ando architecture.

This small museum is almost residential in scale. The three recurrent themes of Ando's architecture appear here: adherence to geometry in organization, use of a limited number of materials, and abstraction of nature. In this museum of contemporary art, Ando uses materials, light, and geometry to create a tranquil place of great spirituality in an urban environment with little legible historical or cultural context. The success of this building in an environment very different from that of Japan demonstrates the universality of Ando's spaces.

Then there are the works by Serra and Kelly. The artists, too, visited the construction site to revise their works and make repeated studies. The completed works occupy the core of the museum. Do contemporary artists object to the art museum as an institution, or do they reject their work being placed in a building called an art museum? The works by Serra and Kelly sit quietly, as if there had been no conflict at all. A comparison of this museum and the Chichu Art Museum in Naoshima reveals different collaborative relationships existing today between art and architecture.

Exterior view

Left:
Interior view looking outside

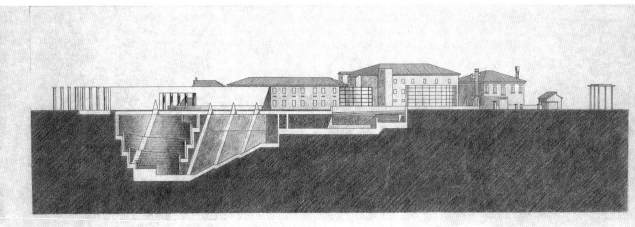

1992–2000 ▸ Fabrica

Benetton Communication Research Center
▸ Treviso, Italy

The oval courtyard

Left page above:
Exterior view
The colonnade of the courtyard creates a
traditional atmosphere.

Left page below:
**The section drawing shows that the new
buildings are installed under the old villa.**

This is an educational research facility that accepts young people from all over the
world to study in many different fields of applied art, such as architecture, design,
photography, graphics, film, textiles, woodwork, metalwork and ceramics. It includes
research rooms, workshops, studios, a gallery, an auditorium, a restaurant, a cafeteria,
and a library where, it is hoped, cultural exchange and face-to-face communication will
take place.

The site is in a suburb of Treviso, a town 30 kilometers from Venice in northern
Italy. A Palladian villa built in the seventeenth century stands on the site. The building
project was conditional on the restoration and preservation of this villa. The relationship between an old building and a new facility is important in a preservation project.
Ando was asked to make full use of the bucolic landscape of this region, to retain the
old villa and to place the new building underground with a sunken court. The elements
of the overall organization are the old villa with a pool in front of it, a colonnaded
gallery that crosses the pool, a two-story-deep elliptical sunken court, and a stepped

outdoor plaza contiguous with the court. The workshops and studios are in the old villa, the library and the gallery face the sunken court, the woodwork and metalwork studios face the stepped plaza. Thus the rooms all face open spaces; the open spaces overlap, leading people from one space to the next. Multiple open spaces arranged on different levels interpenetrate; a complex of spaces is formed from both contrasting and harmoniously continuous elements.

Each element has its own character. A spiral ramp leads to a gallery deep underground. Originally, this was planned as a library for a collection of books relating to art and design. Changes in the program were necessary between planning and realization. The space with a diameter of 66 feet, surrounded by stacks, would no doubt have been a visionary space had it been realized. Ando himself is surrounded by books in his own office; he works at the bottom of a well of books. The Name of the Rose, which takes place in part in a monastic library, is one of his favorite films, and he is fond of the interior landscapes that books create.

The colonnaded gallery crosses the pool and penetrates the old villa. The old villa is reflected in the pool and, overlapping with the new colonnade, gives rise to a new landscape. The landscape in which the real and mirror images of the old villa and the new colonnade overlap is symbolic of the theme of this project—preservation and restoration.

Interior view with skylight

Left page above:
The oval courtyard resembles a sundial.

In projects involving the preservation of an old building, Ando has frequently either buried the new building underground or created contrast by allowing the new element to penetrate the old building. In this bucolic landscape in northern Italy, however, he developed a new design vocabulary of colonnades and elliptical plazas and transformed the entire site into the equivalent of an atmospheric landscape painting.

Luciano Benetton, the client, has explained why he commissioned Ando for this project. "This project required sensitivity toward both the restoration of a villa that is a historical legacy and the creation of a facility oriented to the future. I believed that Ando would not simply restore the old building but carry out a courageous renovation which would serve as a bridge to the future." Benetton states that he was drawn to Ando's simple, Eastern style of architecture. Ando, however, speaks practically no English. How did he establish a relationship of trust with the client? "[Ando] made me feel privileged. He convinced me through nonverbal communication. Ultimately, I may have handed him this project because I wanted to share the experience with him."

Left page below:
Exterior view with columns

1994–1995 · Meditation Space, UNESCO
Paris, France

Left page:
Exterior view with UNESCO building by Marcel Breuer in the background

Right:
The structure of the roof

UNESCO celebrated its 50th anniversary in 1995. To commemorate that event, it was decided to construct a place of prayer for world peace that transcends religious and ethnic distinctions. The site is at UNESCO headquarters, near the Eiffel Tower in Paris. The headquarters is a well-known work of modern architecture designed by Marcel Breuer; there are works of by Picasso, Giacometti and other artists inside and outside the building. Among these works is a Japanese garden designed by Isamu Noguchi. Noguchi was a sculptor who was, by birth and in spirit, both American and Japanese. The garden, however, was in bad repair. A site next to the garden was chosen for the place of prayer. It was a difficult site—Ando had to create an autonomous prayer space expressing a strong idea on a site surrounded by a Breuer building and next to a Japanese garden by Noguchi.

The "Meditation Garden" as a whole is composed of simple elements: two walls to separate the site from the surrounding environment; a terraced pool extending over the entire site; a cylindrical prayer space floating on the pool; and a ramp providing

access to the space. The prayer space is a cylinder 21 feet in diameter and 21 feet in height. The only openings in the cylinder are the two entrances and the skylight. There are no doors, windows or finishes; the space consists only of light and exposed concrete. The bottom of the pool is laid with stones exposed to the atomic bombing of Hiroshima that were donated by that city. Water flows over the stones and symbolically purifies the souls of those who have died in war; the design is a direct expression of a pure desire for peace.

Donations of 10,000 yen (about US$ 88,50) per person were solicited from private individuals in Japan, the only country ever to suffer the effects of atomic bombs, and 140 million yen (about US$ 1,2 million) in all was collected. The names of the donors are recorded on one side of the space; a portion of the funds was set aside for repairing and annually maintaining the garden by Noguchi.

Right page:
Interior view, including four armchairs designed by Ando

1994–2004 ▸ Langen Foundation
Hombroich, Neuss

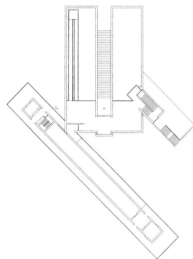

Plan

The story of the Langen Foundation began in an encounter with an ardent lover of art. There is an art museum called the Hombroich Museum Island by the River Erft outside the German city of Neuss near Düsseldorf. This unique museum occupies an entire island in extensive marshland. Scattered across 20 hectares, a dozen or so handsome exhibition pavilions designed by the sculptor Erwin Heerich, together with sculptures in the open air, blend into the surrounding trees. Superb artworks are casually displayed where they can be touched by hand. Hombroich Museum Island is truly a paradise of art. Karl-Heinrich Müller, the owner of this museum, acquired land around the site and, through enormous effort that involved changing the shape of the land and replanting trees, restored it to the state it was several centuries ago. We cannot but be amazed by Müller's imagination and lifelong dedication.

Müller conceived a plan to transform a former NATO missile base about a kilometer northwest of Hombroich Island into an art museum and commissioned Ando to design the gallery. That was the beginning of the Langen Foundation project.

Ando first visited the site in 1994. The museum was completed ten years later. During that time, responsibility for the administration of the museum passed from Karl-Heinrich Müller to the Hombroich Museum Island Foundation. In 2000, the collector Marianne Langen offered to finance the construction. Land was leased from the foundation; construction, restarted in 2002, was at last completed. Marianne Langen was already 90 at the time, but Ando was profoundly impressed by her resolute attitude and decisiveness.

This museum is intended to house and exhibit a collection of Eastern and contemporary art built up by Mrs Langen and her husband. In response to the program, Ando designed two different spaces: a still space filled with soft light for Eastern art and a dynamic space for contemporary art.

Right page above:
Exterior view

Right page below:
Interior view of gallery space

View through the window

The permanent exhibition is displayed in a space with a double-membrane structure: a concrete box inside a glass box. Special exhibitions are held in two spaces buried in the ground at a 45-degree angle relative to the double-membrane structure.

The permanent exhibition of Eastern art is in the box-within-a-box. It is surrounded by a buffer zone similar to the *engawa* (veranda) found in traditional Japanese architecture. There is such continuity between inside and outside that inside the buffer zone we feel as if we were walking in the forest.

The special exhibition buildings are buried in the ground; dramatic light is introduced through skylights into the closed-off gallery, creating a dynamic space. Contrasting spaces, one still and the other dynamic, are created through the drama of light.

Ando was deeply moved by the dream to which Müller and Langen had dedicated their lives. Wishing their dream eternal life, he designed the Langen Foundation so that it blends quietly into the forest. This is a building that is the product of the strong will of Marianne Langen, the energy of Karl-Heinrich Müller, and their love of art. Unfortunately, Marianne Langen died before the museum opened in February 2004. Following her wishes, her daughter, Sabine Langen-Crasemann, now serves as the director of the museum.

1997–2002 ▸ Modern Art Museum

Fort Worth, Texas, USA

Left page:
Reflections of the outer glass shell

Sketch of Y-shaped column

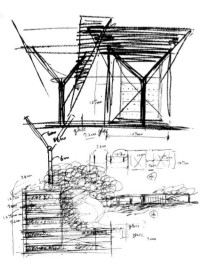

In 1993, Ando was commissioned to design two museums: the Modern Art Museum of Fort Worth in Forth Worth, Texas, U.S.A., and Hyogo Prefectural Museum of Art in Kobe, Japan. In both works, he wrapped concrete boxes in boxes of glass. Ando calls this a new model in his architectural vocabulary.

The Forth Worth museum began as a limited competition. The question was how to give character to an extensive site and how to relate the museum to the Kimbell Art Museum by Louis Kahn across the street. Ando took note of the spatial order characteristic of Kahn's architecture and endowed the entire site with a rhythmical order through the repetition of box-shaped spatial units arranged in parallel. Moreover, observing how Kahn created a solemn light in his building, Ando created a filtered light by using two skins, one of glass and the other of concrete. Furthermore, the light is reflected by the pool, so that a beautiful scene composed of real and virtual images extends to the outdoor space.

The pool was proposed by Ando to meet the competition's objective, which was to create an environment for art surrounded by water and trees. Texas has an arid climate, and water and greenery were necessary if the large site was to be transformed into an oasis of art. Water is a basic element necessary for the creation of an environment friendly to human beings. At the same time, a surface of water, as well as vertical surfaces of glass, are able to transform a site into a Euclidean space. Reflected by the pool, the concrete boxes and glass boxes repeatedly shift in parallel or are reversed in image, depicting transparent, multi-dimensional figures in the water.

The glass walls of Fort Worth have three meanings. First, there is the freezing effect of transparent glass boxes. When a building made of concrete is sealed in an enormous envelope of glass, it is instantaneously frozen, as if it had been enclosed in ice. A glass box freezes not only space but time. That is, by stopping time, it transforms an instant into eternity. A frozen space seems to have the qualities of the classical ideal described by the archaeologist and art historian Johann Joachim Winckelmann (1717–1768) as "quiet grandeur" and "noble simplicity." A concrete box sealed by glass is like a specimen of contemporary architecture displayed in the manner of an archaeological discovery. The way glass freezes time is of course analogous to the function of a museum.

The second effect of glass is to switch the inside and outside of space. Wrapping the concrete box in a glass box reverses inside and outside. A wall that was the outside becomes the inside when wrapped in glass. The glass box also creates a buffer zone. It stabilizes the interior environment within the concrete box and serves a role much like that of the traditional *engawa* (veranda) by assimilating views of the water and greenery. The pool in front of the museum was made somewhat deeper out of consideration for the environment, and the roof extends out over the pool. This serves to mitigate the harsh climatic conditions in the region.

The third function of the glass box is to serve as an emphatic indicator. To present something in a glass box is much like Nietzsche's cry to look at a building. The honor

Entrance hall with large painting by the
German artist Anselm Kiefer

Right:
Gallery space with the work by Anselm Kiefer,
entitled "Book with Wings", 1992–1994
The isolated space enhances the strength of the
work.

The gallery space with glass box extending into the water

Plan of the first floor

of being chosen is underlined by enclosure in a glass box. That is indeed Ando's intention. The function of the glass box is to designate what is enclosed as something separate, that is, to endow the once-only, contingent act called architecture with historical character and inevitability. This separateness and inevitability are indeed special characteristics of Ando's buildings.

1999–2004 ▸ Chichu Art Museum and Art House Project
Naoshima, Kagawa

The sharp edged corner does not follow the perpendicular line.

Japanese architects tend not to tamper with land. However Ando is not loathe to shape land. He placed importance on site planning even as a young architect but has gradually grown bolder in manipulating topography since the Koshino House. In Rokko Housing, he took up the challenge of a steep hillside; in Suntory Museum, he used a seaside site to create a new relationship between the sea and architecture. Twenty years later, in the Chichu Art Museum, he created a dramatic museum of art by burying geometrical forms beneath a mountainside.

Naoshima is a small island in the Inland Sea. Ando has been involved with this island for well over ten years. Although the Chichu Art Museum is located on a hill on the island, the building is buried completely in the ground out of consideration for the natural scenery of the Inland Sea. The museum as a whole is composed of galleries organized around two courtyards, one an equilateral triangle and the other a square in plan, and the open-air passageways linking those galleries. Underground, axes and directions do not exist. That is precisely why strong forms, unique materials and artists of a passionate nature are demanded in spaces below ground.

Chichu Art Museum is dedicated to the permanent exhibition of works by three men, the Impressionist Claude Monet and the contemporary artists Walter de Maria and James Turrell. To put it another way, this is a house where artworks are to reside permanently; the architecture and the artworks cannot be considered separately. In the Turrell space, we are in close contact with the sky. We also experience the creation of a cube in mid-air of white light. In the Walter de Maria room, a work placed on the wall of an enormous staircase radiates a golden color and creates a space with a religious atmosphere. In the Monet room, plastered walls with rounded corners and a floor paved with marble create the impression that we are encountering the water lilies of Monet somewhere in outer space. In other art museums, artworks are things to be looked at; in this museum, however, artworks are things to be experienced with our entire bodies. Naturally, it would not be possible to experience the works in this way without the help of the architectural space. Looked at another way, the Chichu Art Museum is an underground laboratory. This is an ambitious attempt to create spaces where visitors can experience the works in a pure way, using the underground environment. We are cut off from the outside world; our perceptions are made sensitive; we are able to concentrate solely on looking at the artworks. This is a bold concept.

Right:
Section

Left page:
The natural landscape remains since no buildings appear on the ground level.

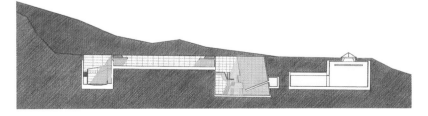

The client, Soichiro Fukutake, is one of the leading collectors of contemporary art in
Japan. He commissions works, mainly to be prepared on Naoshima, by artists invited
from around the world. In 1998 the Art House Project was initiated in the village of
Motomura, on the east side of the island. This is a project to restore and preserve
traditional folk-houses remaining in the village and use them as galleries for permanent exhibitions of contemporary art. The idea of rebuilding unoccupied houses in
an old community on Naoshima and creating small art museums throughout the town
is an interesting one.

One such museum is Minami-Dera, designed by Ando for James Turrell. It is a
windowless building, with a dark space which no light from outside penetrates.
Turrell's work "Backside of the Moon" emerges out of the darkness. There is in that
darkness a minuscule amount of white light. Ando created a space of darkness that
rejects light, and Turrell introduced an extremely small amount of light into that
darkness to demonstrate how, in darkness, even a spoonful of light can serve as an
eloquent critique and change the meaning of the world.

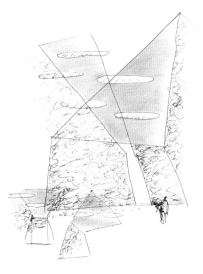

Right:
Room for Claude Monet
The position of the water lilies painting is a little bit lower than usual but very effective.

Left page below:
Image sketch of the relation between sky and underground

2001–2003 ▸ 4 x 4 House

Kobe, Hyogo

View from the roadside
In the beginning there was only one house.

Left page:
View from the seaside
At night the house appears like a lighthouse.

Dimensions and geometry explain the house's name.

This is an extremely small private house standing on the coast of the Inland Sea in Japan. Eroded by the sea, much of the site is under water. The site is unique. Regulations regarding shore protection limited construction to a small, 16.5 foot-square space. The biggest problem was creating ample living space on the extremely small site. The more difficult the problem, the more interesting Ando's solution is likely to be. This is an example of Ando's style of humor. Confronted with a difficult task, he was able to create a building unlike anything we have seen before. A Japanese periodical called "Brutus" (published by MAGAZINEHOUSE) invited persons interested in asking Ando to design a building to submit possible sites. This unique site was chosen by Ando himself from the various submissions.

Ando has taken a plan, 13 feet by 13 feet (4 m x 4 m)—the maximum dimensions possible for the site—and created a four-story tower. The entrance and utility room are on the first floor, a bedroom is on the second floor, a study is on the third floor and the living/ dining room (the heart of the house) is on the top floor. The extremely small site permitted nothing elaborate; the organization is simple and clear. The stairway occupies a large percentage of the floor space, especially since each floor is only 13 foot-square. However, the stairway takes up only half the space on the top floor since there is no need for it to go any higher. Advantage was taken of this fact to displace the topmost floor by three feet and give the kitchen and living area more space. Here, too, we can see Ando work his particular magic—the transformation of the accidental into the inevitable.

The topmost floor is a cube, four meters to a side, that is pushed out toward the sea. The seaward side is completely glazed; the view is such that we feel as if we were out on the sea on a boat. The space allows us to fully enjoy the wide expanse of the sea and the sky. It corroborates Ando's assertion that expansiveness of space has nothing to do with the size of a building.

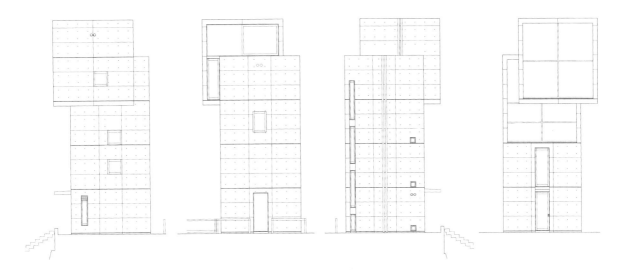

Since its completion, Ando has published a scheme for an addition to this building. The addition is a glass box on the beach that becomes submerged by the sea at full tide. It is a poetic proposal. However, Ando has in fact built a house of the same shape next to this building. It is the same in shape yet different—a twin but made of a different material. The two houses of the same form, one concrete and the other wooden, have great impact on the coastal landscape.

In his younger days, Ando published a project called Twin Wall; he has also built a house called Soseikan (literally "Twin Residence"—also known as the Yamaguchi House). If the Row House in Sumiyoshi is a work with a powerful monistic character, Ando has from time to time also used similar, twinned forms for windows and ducting and created dualistic works. Here, however, he has given the two houses, arranged side by side, such similar forms that a seascape of a kind with which we are all familiar is transformed into a surrealistic landscape. Is this an instance of Andoesque humor, or is it meant as a symbol of the fact that Ando is himself one of twin brothers?

View from the shoreline with the house

Interior view of kitchen/dining room on the top floor

Left:
View of 2004
The two buildings have the same size and the same form, but are built of different materials.

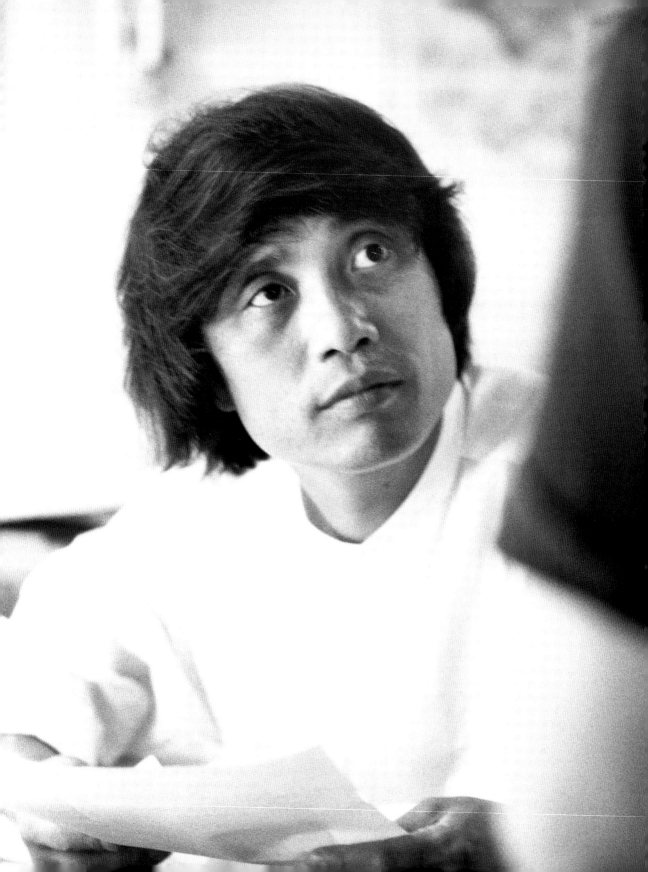

Life and work

1941 ▶ Born in Osaka, Japan. One of twin brothers, he is raised by his maternal grandmother. They live by themselves in a deep, narrow two-story row house of wooden construction. His grandmother is his most important mentor.

1955 ▶ Raised in a neighborhood of low-income row houses, shops and small factories. After school hours, he frequents a carpenter's shop and a glass factory nearby and learns the importance of craftsmanship. At the age of 14, he builds a small shed for a friend. The streets are for him an extension of school.

1958 ▶ Makes his debut as a professional boxer at 17. He acquires a boxing license and goes to Thailand to fight. His experience as a professional boxer will have the biggest influence on his life. 50 years later, he will still train and exercise every night.

1959 ▶ At the age of 18, he is commissioned to design the interior of a nightclub.

1960 ▶ Explores traditional temples and tea houses in Kyoto and Osaka in his early 20s. He has decided to educate himself through physical experience rather than schooling.

1965 ▶ Travels around the world to educate himself in architecture at 24. On the first leg of his journey, he goes to Moscow via the Trans-Siberian Railway and tours European capitals. Years later, he will still have vivid memories of Siberia, the Indian Ocean and the Ganges River. He calls this his Grand Tour.

1969 ▶ Establishes his own office in Osaka after traveling all over the world for four years. His office becomes an exciting salon for young architects. He marries Yumiko Kato, then an assistant in his office.

1973 ▶ Designs the Tomishima House in Osaka for his friend. He will later purchase this house and use it as his architectural office.

1976 ▶ Completes his *magnum opus*, the Row House in Sumiyoshi, Osaka. The house is quite small but expresses his determination to reform society through architecture.

1979 ▶ Awarded the annual prize from the Architectural Institute of Japan.

At the opening of the one-man exhibition at MoMA, N.Y., with Philip Johnson, 1991

1980 ▶ Completes the Koshino House. Four years later, he will add a circular atelier to the two concrete boxes. 25 years later, he will renovate the spatial organization once more. Long-lasting relationships based on trust exist between him and his clients.

1983 ▶ Completes Rokko Housing I in Kobe. It stands on a steep slope commanding a view of Kobe and the Osaka Bay area. The choice of location is bold but critical to the design. It will come through the Hanshin-Awaji earthquake undamaged, demonstrating its safety and sturdiness.

1984 ▶ Completes Time's I, a commercial complex shaped like a ship on the bank of a river surrounded by an exquisite old townscape.

1985 ▶ Awarded the 5th Alvar Aalto Medal by the Finnish Association of Architects. In subsequent years he will receive most of the world's great architectural prizes and medals.

1986 ▶ Completes Chapel on Mt. Rokko in Kobe, sometimes called the Chapel of the Winds. He will subsequently create many masterpieces of religious architecture. He also completes the Kidosaki House in Tokyo, whose astonishingly beautiful spaces are in marked contrast to those of the Row House in Sumiyoshi.

1987–1990 ▶ Serves as visiting professor at Yale, Columbia and Harvard Universities.

1988 ▶ Completes Church on the Water in Hokkaido.

1989 ▶ Awarded the Gold Medal of Architecture by the French Academy of Architecture. He completes Church of the Light in Osaka.

1991 ▶ Completes Water Temple Hompuku-ji in Hyogo Prefecture.

1992 ▶ Completes the Japan Pavilion for Expo '92 in Seville. This enormous wooden structure is an integration of traditional Japanese culture and contemporary technology. He completes Naoshima Contemporary Art Museum; in 1995 he will build an Annex including a small oval hotel with a pond on a hilltop site.

1993 ▶ Awarded the Carlsberg Architectural Prize, Denmark.
He completes Rokko Housing II in Kobe.

1994 ▶ Completes the Chikatsu-Asuka Historical Museum in Osaka and the Museum of Wood in Hyogo Prefecture.

1995 ▶ Awarded the Asahi Prize, Japan, and the Pritzker Architecture Prize, USA.
Completes the Meditation Space for UNESCO in Paris.
The Hanshin-Awaji earthquake strikes on January 17, causing great damage on his home ground. All his works come through unscathed. He extends help to people and buildings that have suffered from the disaster. At the Pritzker Prize ceremony, he proposes the establishment of a foundation to support any child who has lost a parent in the disaster and contributes the prize money to the foundation.

1996 ▶ Organizes the Hyogo Green Network, which will plant 250,000 trees with white flowers in memory of those who died in the disaster.

1997 ▶ Awarded the Royal Gold Medal of the Royal Institute of British Architects, UK. He is appointed professor at the University of Tokyo. He publishes a book of his lectures, "Rensen Renpai" (Successive Battles, Successive Defeats), dealing with his life and architecture, which becomes a bestseller among students, businessmen and housewives.

1999 ▶ Completes Rokko Housing III in Kobe. His beloved dog, Corbusier, named after his hero, dies, to the couple's great sorrow. The dog lived in the office and was like a member of the family. Ando has always loved animals and as a child used to take a dog to elementary school with him.

2000 ▶ Completes Komyo-ji Temple in Saijo and Fabrica in Treviso, Italy.

Planting acorns for campaign "Setouchi Olive Foundation" with children, 2001

He establishes the Seto Inland Sea Olive Network Foundation. As leader of the campaign, he visits small islands that have been damaged by industrial pollution. His aim is to work with local children for the elimination of pollution. His involvement in civic activities and concern for environmental issues arise from his architectural work on Naoshima.

2001 ▸ Completes the Pulitzer Foundation for the Arts in St. Louis, USA.

2002 ▸ Awarded the Gold Medal of the American Institute of Architects, and The Kyoto Prize, Japan.
Completes the Modern Art Museum of Fort Worth, USA. This project, the subject of an international competition, is across the street from the Kimbell Art Museum, Louis Kahn's masterpiece.

2003 ▸ Completes the 4 x 4 House in Kobe. Two years later, he will build another 4 x 4 house on an adjacent site. These two houses are like twins; they are similar in size and design but made of different materials for different clients.

2004 ▸ Completes Chichu Art Museum in Naoshima. Chichu is "underground" in Japanese. Since Nakanoshima Project II—Space Strata (1988), Ando has a dream of creating architecture underground. The client of this private museum is one of the leading modern art collectors in Japan. Langen Foundation created in Germany for a modern art collector who has left a lasting impression on Ando and played an important role in the completion of the facility.

2005 ▸ Awarded the Gold Medal of Union Internationale des Architectes, Paris.

Japan

Ashiya, Hyogo
Koshino House

Ibaraki, Osaka
Church of the Light

Kobe, Hyogo
Rokko Housing I, II, III, IV
4 x 4 House

Mikata, Hyogo
Museum of Wood

Minamikawachi, Osaka
Chikatsu-Asuka Historical Museum

Naoshima, Kagawa
Chichu Art Museum
Naoshima Contemporary Art Museum

Saijo, Ehime
Komyo-ji Temple

Setagaya-ku, Tokyo
Kidosaki House

Sumiyoshi, Osaka
Row House

Tsuna, Hyogo
Water Temple Hompuku-ji

Yufutsu, Hokkaido
Church on the Water

Yufutsu

SEA OF JAPAN

JAPAN

Tokyo

Mikata

Ashiya   Ibaraki
Kobe   Osaka
Naoshima
Tsuna   Minamikawachi

Saijo

PACIFIC OCEAN

Worldmap

NORTH AMERICA

St. Louis
New York
Washington
rt Worth

ATLANTIC OCEAN

London
Berlin
Neuss
Weil am Rhein
Paris
Treviso
EUROPE
Madrid
Roma
Sevilla

AFRICA

Fort Worth, Texas, USA
Modern Art Museum of Fort Worth

Neuss, Germany
Langen Foundation

Paris, France
Meditation Space, UNESCO

Seville, Spain
Expo '92

St. Louis, Missouri, USA
Pulitzer Foundation for the Arts

Treviso, Italy
Fabrica

Weil am Rhein, Germany
Vitra seminar house

Bibliography

► Emilio Ambasz, Tadao Ando: Intercepting Light, Urban Center Books, 1985, New York
► Tadao Ando minimalisme, Electa Moniteur, 1982, Paris
► Ando Tadao (Gendai no Kenchikuka), Kajima Institute Publishing, 1982, Tokyo
► Tadao Ando. Obras y proyectos. 1972–1982, Museo Espanõl de Arte Contemporáneo, 1982, Madrid
► Tadao Ando. The Yale Studio & Current Works, Rizzoli, 1989, New York
► Tadao Ando, Architectural Monographs 14, Academy Editions / St. Martin's Press, 1990, London / New York
► Tadao Ando. Album de l'exposition, Centre Georges Pompidou, 1993, Paris
► Tadao Ando Lectures at the University of Tokyo, University of Tokyo Press / China Architecture & Building Press, 1999, Tokyo / Beijing
► Tadao Ando, Tadao Ando 1993–2000. El croquis 44 + 58, El Croquis Editorial, 2000, Madrid
► Tadao Ando, Losing Battles, After Battles. Tadao Ando Lectures at the University of Tokyo 2, University of Tokyo Press, 2001, Tokyo
► Ando Tadao Museum Guide, Bijutsu Shuppan-Sha, 2001, Tokyo
► Tadao Ando, Light and Water, The Monacelli Press, 2003, New York
► Michael Auping, Seven Interviews with Tadao Ando, Modern Art Museum of Fort Worth, 2002, London
► Pascal Bertrand, Tadao Ando et la maison Koshino, Mardaga, 1990, Liège
► Werner Blaser (ed.), Tadao Ando, Sketches – Zeichnungen, Birkhäuser Verlag, 1990, Basel
► Werner Blaser (ed.), Tadao Ando. Architektur der Stille, Birkhäuser Verlag, 2001, Basel
► William J. R. Curtis, Beyond Minimalism. The Architecture of Tadao Ando, Royal Academy of Arts (ed.), 1998, London
► Francesco Dal Co, Tadao Ando. Le opere, gli scritti, la critica, Electa, 1994, Milan
► Francesco Dal Co, Tadao Ando. Complete Works, Phaidon Press, 1995, London
► Philip Drew, Church on the Water and Church of the Light, Phaidon Press, 1996, London
► Kenneth Frampton (ed.), Tadao Ando. Buildings, Projects, Writings, Rizzoli, 1984, New York
► Masao Furuyama, Tadao Ando, Birkhäuser Verlag, 1995, Basel
► Yukio Futagawa (ed.), Architecture Method / Kenchiku Shuho, A.D.A. EDITA Tokyo, 2005, Tokyo
► Takeshi Ishido (ed.), Hikari no Kyokai. Ando Tadao no Genba, Kenchiku Shiryo Kenkyusha, 2000, Tokyo
► Kobun Ito (ed.), Gendai no Kenchikuka Tadao Ando II 1981–1989, Kajima Institute Publishing, 1990, Tokyo
► Philip Jodidio, Ando. Complete Works, Taschen, 2004, Cologne
► Kazukiyo Matsuba, Ando. Architect, Kodansha International, 1998, Tokyo / New York
► Kazuo Nishi, Tadao Ando. Beyond Horizons in Architecture, in: Kenchiku bunka 550, pp. 93–96, Tadao Ando Exhibition Committe, 1992, Tokyo / Osaka
► Yann Nussaume, Tadao Ando et la question du milieu. Réflexions sur l'architecture et le paysage, Éditions Le Moniteur, 1999, Paris
► Kazuo Ogura (ed.), Ando Tadao. Chohatsusuru hako, Maruzen, 1986, Tokyo
► Richard Pare, The colours of light. Tadao Ando architecture, Phaidon Press, 1996, London
► Anatxu Zabalbeascoa, Javier Rodríguez Marcos, Tadao Ando. Architecture and spirit, Editorial Gustavo Gili, 1998, Barcelona

Credits

The Author

Masao FURUYAMA
► 1947 Born in Kyoto
► 1971 Graduate from Kyoto University, Architecture Department
► 1976 Dr. of Engineering from Tokyo University, Urban Engineering
► 1990 Professor of Kyoto Institute of Technology
► 2004 Vice-President of Kyoto Institute of Technology